THE
SEVEN FEASTS
OF ISRAEL

BY

ZOLA LEVITT

Lev. 23

ZOLA LEVITT

Zola Levitt is a Jewish believer thoroughly educated in the synagogues and brought to the Messiah in 1971. He holds degrees from Duquesne University, Indiana University and an honorary Th.D. from Faith Bible College. He has, in his Christian walk, addressed millions of people concerning the facts of the Bible through his national television program, **ZOLA LEVITT PRESENTS,** which is carried on the major Christian networks, CBN, PTL, TBN and LBN, and numerous large city broadcast stations.

Zola Levitt Ministries, Inc. is a teaching and evangelistic association guided by the standard of Rom. 1:16, "To the Jew first, and also to the Gentile." Like the apostle Paul, we work through the Gentiles to reach the Jews. We inform our Gentile viewers and listeners of those principles of the faith which will be most helpful to them in understanding and witnessing to their Jewish friends. Our ministry offers a wide variety of teaching materials including books, cassette tapes, music, video tapes, and some imported gift items from the Holy Land. A current list of these materials is available at no charge by writing to: ZOLA, Box 12268, Dallas, TX 75225.

I
THE SEVEN FEASTS
OF ISRAEL

It is with a feeling of humility and hopelessness that a writer attempts to explain the seven feasts of Israel. God has established an infinitely meaningful and profound prophetic system through His choices of seven holy convocations to be held each year by the Chosen People. He dictated the dates and proper observances to Moses on Mount Sinai, and His instructions are recorded in the chapter Leviticus 23.

Indeed a book the size of the entire Bible itself would be needed to fully expound Lev. 23 and the momentous results of its symbolism. The events of the New Testament, the vital future events involving the Church and the Jews — indeed, all of God's plan from chaos to eternity — are ingeniously revealed through the nature of timing of these seven annual feasts. The reader will become aware that we are now existing, as it were, between two feasts, and that it is ultimately important for us to comprehend God's calendar in its essence.

It should be noted that God was very practical in issuing the seven feasts within one brief chapter of instruction. They are mentioned elsewhere in Scripture, but these vital and fundamental requirements of the Old Covenant were gathered together in simplest form lest no one overlook any of them. If there was one chapter of the entire Old Testament that the faithful Jew would want to remember, it is this one. An error in the celebration of the seven feasts — even just an error in the celebration of the Day of Atonement, the sixth one — would result in banishment from the Chosen People!

The feasts are celebrated today in altered forms by the Jews who wish to follow the Old Covenant as closely as possible; however, since their major feature was sacrifice, and since sacrifice is impossible without the proper Temple of God in Jerusalem, the original meaning and efficacy of the feasts has been completely lost. And without a knowledge of the New Testament, even the fulfillments of the feasts—the most far reaching and momentous features of their meanings—are lost.

Believers in Christ are not responsible to keep these feasts, of course, but a knowledge of them greatly enhances their faith. The Lord kept every one of them without fail, even celebrating Passover on His last earthly night.

Below we will examine each feast individually, giving the appropriate verse from Leviticus 23. In each case we will see that there is a wonderful fulfillment in the New Testament as indicated by the nature of the feast.

PASSOVER

The festival year begins with Passover, to be held at the beginning of spring:

> In the fourteenth day of the first month at even is the Lord's passover (Lev. 23:5).

The Lord gives but a single verse to the direction for Passover, since the children of Israel and Moses had, in effect, recently celebrated it. Exodus 12 and the ensuing chapters tell the monumental story of the national liberation from Egypt, marked by the terrible night of the tenth plague. God merely assigns Passover its date, but thereby hangs a fascinating concept.

God's calendar is a lunar calendar based on the phases of the moon rather than the earth's revolutions around the sun. Each month starts with a new moon, reaching a full moon in the midst of the twenty-eight day cycle. Thus Passover always falls on a full moon — the first full moon of spring. The approximate twenty-eight day lunar cycle is harmonious throughout nature; the tides of the seas rise and fall with the moon and even the menstrual cycle seems to obey this particular time cycle. The moon makes for a much better calendar than the sun, of course, since it changes every night. Those accustomed to a lunar calendar would estimate on any clear night what day of the month it was. The sun, of course, does not change daily. We see it whole or we don't see it at all. God may not have preferred the use of the sun for men's calendars since sun worship, as practiced profusely in Egypt, was inevitably the leading form of paganism. Irreverent men seemed captivated by the magnificence of the sun and thus tended to worship the created object rather than the Creator. In Hebrew reckoning, the day begins at sundown, or moonrise. This seemed to be God's intention at the very beginning ("And the evening and the morning were the first day," Gen. 1:5).

The almond tree blooms at the end of winter with a most noticeable flowing of white blossoms. This encouraging act of nature in a bleak season is alluded to in the Scriptures. We should appreciate that even if an individual could not read, or could not even comprehend a calendar, he would still not omit Passover. All that was necessary was for him to notice the blooming of the almond blossoms. The next full moon was the first feast. All of the other feasts are based back on Passover or on a simple numbering of days from a given point.

Back to the meaning of Passover; it is surely the feast of salvation. On this day, because of the blood of the lamb ("without blemish, a male . . ." Exodus 12:5) the Hebrew nation was delivered from bondage. Clearly, in both Testaments, the blood of the Lamb delivers from slavery — the Jew from Egypt, the Christian from sin.

It is no mere coincidence, then, that our Lord Himself was sacrificed on Passover. At the meal He stated plainly, "This is

My blood of the New Testament shed for many for remission of sin" (Matthew 26:27). John the Baptist clearly marked out the person of Jesus Christ as a blood sacrifice when he stated, "Behold the Lamb of God, which taketh away the sin of the world" (John 1:29).

The Christian celebrates Passover, in effect, by participating in the sacrifice of the Lord. Back in Egypt the Jew marked his house with the blood of the lamb. Today the Christian marks his house — his body, "the house of the spirit" — with the blood of Christ. The Angel of Death will pass over each Christian as surely as he passed over each Israelite in Egypt. We are already living our eternal life.

The remarkable fulfillment of Passover on the exact day illustrates a principle which we will see with each of the feasts. Our Lord fulfilled each feast on its appropriate day with an appropriate action up to the point we have now reached in His prophetic plan. We will see that all seven of the feasts have either been fulfilled, or are prophesied to be fulfilled, with reference to their exact meanings.

Passover, then, represents our salvation. We do not keep the feast in remembrance of the exodus from Egypt, since that was the mere shadow of the greater redemption to come. The Lord Himself instructed us to "Do this in remembrance of Me." We do take communion, a part of the original Passover feast, in remembrance of the Lord (See "The Miracle of Passover", another of the books in this series, for the beautiful meanings of the bread and wine as established at the Lord's own Passover table).

UNLEAVENED BREAD

The second feast begins on the next night:

> And on the fifteenth day of the same month is the feast of unleavened bread unto the Lord: seven days ye must

eat unleavened bread (Lev. 23:6).

God told the Jews to eat only the pure unleavened bread during the week following Passover. Leaven in the Bible symbolized sin and evil. Unleavened bread, eaten over a period of time (seven days), symbolized a holy walk, as with the Lord. The apostle Paul commented beautifully on the feast of Passover and Unleavened Bread, with which he was, of course, quite familiar as a Jewish scholar:

> Purge out therefore the old leaven, that ye may be a new lump, as ye are unleavened. For even Christ our passover is sacrificed for us: Therefore let us keep the feast, not with old leaven, neither with the leaven of malice and wickedness; but with the unleavened bread of sincerity and truth (I Cor. 5:7-8).

The unleavened bread in the New Testament is, of course, the body of our Lord. He is described as "the Bread of Life". He was born in Bethlehem, in Hebrew "House of Bread". He utilized bread as an image of Himself ("If a kernel of wheat fall into the ground . . ."). God fed the Israelites in the wilderness with manna from heaven, and He feeds the Christians in the world on the Bread of Life. The very piece of bread used by the Jews during this week of Unleavened Bread is a good picture of our Lord. Anyone who has seen the Jewish matzoh sees that it is striped ("By His stripes are we healed"), pierced ("They shall look upon me whom they've pierced"), and, of course, pure, without any leaven, as His body was without any sin. The Passover ceremony of breaking and burying and then resurrecting a piece of this bread (the middle piece, as the Son in the Trinity) very obviously presents the Gospel in the midst of the modern Jewish Passover celebration.

God performed this exact ceremony with the burial of Jesus, our precious piece of unleavened bread, and more importantly, He performed it on the exact day of the feast. Once again,

the required feast was fulfilled in a remarkable and un-
mistakable way.

We readily see from the Gospel that Jesus was buried at
the beginning of the Feast of Unleavened Bread since His body
was interred at sundown of Passover Day, the beginning of
the fifteenth of Nisan, the first month. Our "kernel of wheat"
was indeed placed into the ground, and at the appropriate
moment. It was to rise again, of course, and again in accordance with the schedule of the feasts, as we shall see. One
cannot permanently bury a Christian.

Men have speculated just how it was that Jesus died so
quickly on the cross. Crucifixion normally took three days.
That was the point of it. The victim died by inches as the people passed the cross, morning and night, morning and night.
The Romans utilized this slow and terrible way of death to ter-
rify the population of provincial Israel. We see in the Gospel
that the centurion was not ready to believe that the young,
strong Carpenter of Galilee was dead in just six hours. The
speculation is ended of course, if we simply understand the
schedule of the first two feasts. Our Lord died in time to be
buried at sundown that day. He was placed on the cross at
9:00 a.m. ("The third hour") and taken down at 3:00 p.m.
There was then time enough to wrap the body and bury it
at sundown. The answer to why He died in six hours is that's
all the time He could spare. Our Lord never omitted a feast.
He said pointedly enough that no one could take His life from
Him — "I lay it down and I take it up again."

FIRST FRUITS

The third feast is held on the Sunday following Unleavened Bread:

> Speak unto the children of Israel, and say unto them,
> When ye be come into the land which I give unto you, and

shall reap the harvest thereof, then ye shall bring a sheaf of the firstfruits of your harvest unto the priest: And he shall wave the sheaf before the Lord, to be accepted for you: on the morrow after the sabbath the priest shall wave it (Lev. 23:10-11).

God wanted a special feast during which the Israelites would acknowledge the fertility of the fine land He gave them. They were to bring the early crops of their spring planting ("First Fruits") to the priest at the Temple to be waved before the Lord on their behalf. This was to be done "the morrow after the sabbath," or Sunday. Since the feast of Unleavened Bread was seven days long, one of those days would be a Sunday and that Sunday would be First Fruits each year.

We have come to call this feast Easter, after the Babylonian goddess, Ishtar, the pagan goddess of fertility. We even continue to worship the objects of fertility — the rabbit, the egg, new costumes, etc., but the celebration was to be over God's replanting of the earth in the spring.

We miss a very important biblical truth by not using the term "First Fruits" as the name of this feast, because "first" implies a second, a third, and so on, and that is the real meaning of the feast. We do not merely celebrate the resurrection of the Lord on First Fruits, on which it indeed occurred, but even more so, the resurrection of the entire Church! We shall all be resurrected and go to heaven, just as the Lord did, "Every man in his own order." The apostle Paul presented this brilliantly:

> For as in Adam all die, even so in Christ shall all be made alive. But every man in his own order: Christ the firstfruits; afterward they that are Christ's at his coming (I Cor. 15:23).

Paul makes very clear the real point of the feast. The resurrection of the Lord Himself is happy news indeed, and worthy of a celebration, but we are not so surprised by it. After all, the Lord could raise the dead Himself; He walked on water. He is God's Son. The *real* miracle is that each of us ordinary mortal sinners will experience this resurrection!

We apparently all have a number and will go in that order. Jesus Christ's number was one; He was the First Fruits — the first man permanently resurrected. Your father has a lower number than you, and your grandfather a lower than he, if you were saved in that order. But in any case, we shall *all* go! Obviously, "The dead in Christ shall rise first" (I Thess. 4:16-17) since they have lower numbers.

How simple it all is if we understand these feasts. Jesus of course, celebrated the Sunday of the week of His crucifixion by rising from the dead. It was not some other day He chose but the very day of First Fruits, of course, just as He had performed on Passover and Unleavened Bread, each with the appropriate action. Jesus even presented His proper First Fruits offering to the Father. Graves were opened and dead people rose and were seen after His resurrection in Jerusalem (Matthew 27:53). The Lord, not unlike a Jewish planter, gratefully showed the Father the early crops of what will be a magnificent harvest later on.

First Fruits was the last of the feasts that the Lord was seen personally fulfilling on earth. But His ministry to the Church was to go on, of course, in the ensuing feasts, and again, each on their appropriate days. We now turn to the fourth feast, to be held fifty days after First Fruits.

PENTECOST (or Weeks)

God gave very specific directions for counting the proper number of days until the Feast of Harvest, which we refer to as Pentecost. It actually marked the summer harvest, the second of the year, in which many more crops were available than at First Fruits (but still not as many as would be forthcoming in the great fall harvest):

> And ye shall count unto you from the morrow after sabbath, from the day that ye brought the sheaf of the wave offering; seven sabbaths shall be complete: Even unto the morrow after the seventh sabbath shall ye number fifty days; and ye shall offer a new meat offering unto the Lord (Lev. 23:15-16).

Pentecost, then, occurs on a Sunday, again "The morrow after the sabbath," exactly fifty days after First Fruits. Quite a few directions are given in the following verses in Lev. 23 which are of interest. We have been skipping over the various directions for the feasts, but two verses in particular give us most interesting facts, which show God's careful planning for the future:

> Ye shall bring out of your habitations two wave loaves of two tenth deals; they shall be of fine flour; they shall be baken with leaven; they are the firstfruits unto the Lord (Lev. 23:17).

This subtle instruction indicates a great truth. These two "wave loaves" are of equal weight and they are baked with leaven. They are called "firstfruits". Since they are baked with leaven, they represent sinful man (certainly not, for example, Jesus and the Holy Spirit, who are unleavened) and since they are "firstfruits" they are redeemed or resurrected men. Obviously God was predicting here that the Church would be comprised of two parts, Jew and Gentile. We seem to think of the Church today as entirely Gentile, but of course it has always been part Jewish, since the Lord inevitably retains a remnant of His People. The greater body of Jews will join the Church in the kingdom at the Second Coming (Zechariah 12:10; 13:1) when "All Israel will be saved" (Romans 11:26).

Also interesting in the direction for Pentecost is this peculiar command:

> And when ye reap the harvest of your land, thou shalt not make clean riddance of the corners of thy field when thou reapest, neither shalt thou gather any gleaning of thy harvest: thou shalt leave them unto the poor, and to the stranger: I am the Lord your God (Lev. 23:22).

Some of the poor who ate from the corners of the fields that were left unharvested, according to the law, were Jesus and His men.

The book "The Spirit of Pentecost," another of the books in this series, details this important festival as it occurred in the New Testament. We can give some high points in this space. The Lord, of course, rejoined His disciples after His resurrection and taught them for forty days (Acts 1:3), and then bade them to wait at Jerusalem until the Holy Spirit would come. The Holy Spirit did come exactly on the day of the feast (Acts 2:1) and gathered a harvest of three thousand souls.

How rejuvenating this was to the handful of Christians who waited fearfully on the Lord's promise of a Comforter. Consider Peter, who three times had denied he even knew the Lord only seven weeks before. Now he was able to preach the mighty doctrine of Pentecost, to clearly quote from the prophet Joel and the Psalms, and to bring a massive crowd of Jews to the Messiah.

The fulfillment was exactly in keeping with the purpose of the feast. It was a greater harvest of souls than the Lord had presented at First Fruits, but of course, only a token of the great harvest to come in the Rapture of the Church. The three thousand was a significant number. Exactly that number were killed on the day the law came down from Mount Sinai, because of the golden calf (Exodus 32:28). "The letter kills, the Spirit gives life."

It must have been a major argument of the disciples following Pentecost, as they witnessed to the Jews, that the feasts had been fulfilled in remarkable fashion in that momentous year. Whatever they may have thought previously of the rustic teacher from Galilee, they certainly had to admit that it seemed more than coincidental that He was crucified on Passover, buried on Unleavened Bread, raised on First Fruits, and had sent the Holy Spirit on Pentecost. Four coincidences are hard to explain away, expecially when each one is so completely appropriate to its purpose.

The same situation applies still today, because we have not as yet seen the fulfillment to feast number five. We remain under the orders of Pentecost, continuing the summer crop cultivation. We remain "workers in a field" until that day of the great harvest marked by the next feast.

TRUMPETS

God seems to have enjoyed the trumpet. Ever since Isaac was spared by virtue of the ram being caught in the thicket by its horn, the trumpet, or in biblical times, the ram's horn, was special to God. After all, without Isaac, we would not have had the Jews; and without the Jews, we would not have had the Bible, the apostles, the disciples, and we must suppose, the Messiah Himself.

God actually seemed to enjoy hearing trumpets blown, and He used them to great effect when Joshua conquered Jericho. He also specified their use in the Year of Jubilee (Lev. 25:8-10) having the trumpets "proclaim liberty throughout all the land unto all the inhabitants thereof." That quotation appears today on the Liberty Bell in Philadelphia, and may reassure those who feel this country was not founded by Bible-reading men.

But even previous to Jericho, God instructed Moses about trumpets on Mt. Sinai, in regard to our fifth feast!

> Speak unto the children of Israel, saying, in the seventh
> month, in the first day of the month, shall ye have a sab-
> bath, a memorial of blowing of trumpets, an holy con-
> vocation (Lev. 23:24).

We have skipped over quite a bit of time now from
Pentecost, to picture the year as it was prescribed. Our first
three feasts occurred, of course, in the first month, normally
in April. Pentecost occurred at the early part of summer, usual-
ly in late May or early June. Now we go over to the first day
of Tishrei, on the Jewish calendar, the seventh month, which
occurs in the fall, in September. This jump in time seems to
represent the Church Age in God's planning, since the trumpet
unquestionably represents the Rapture of the Church.

The trumpet was the signal for the field workers to come
into the Temple. The high priest actually stood on the
southwestern parapet of the Temple and blew the trumpet so
that it could be heard in the surrounding fields. At that in-
stant, the faithful would stop harvesting even if there were more
crops to bring in, and leave immediately for the worship ser-
vices. The Lord used the image. We can imagine the scene
as a Jew and an Arab worked side by side in the fields, as
they do even today. When the trumpet would sound, the Jew
would leave immediately, and the Arab, believing otherwise
of course, would continue bringing in the crops. Thus the Lord
stated, "Where there are two working in a field, I'll take one
and leave the other."

The Rapture is very clearly associated with trumpets:

> For the Lord himself shall descend from heaven with a
> shout, with the voice of the archangel, and with the trump
> of God: and the dead in Christ shall rise first: Then we
> which are alive and remain shall be caught up together
> with them in the clouds, to meet the Lord in the air: and
> so shall we ever be with the Lord (I Thess. 4:16-17).

Behold, I shew you a mystery; We shall not all sleep, but we shall all be changed, in a moment, in the twinkling of an eye, at the last trump: for the trumpet shall sound, and the dead shall be raised incorruptible, and we shall be changed (I Cor. 15:51-52).

When that great trumpet sounds, the miracle to surpass all miracles will take place. The living believers will rise from the earth. The graves will give up their dead. All the believers will be mysteriously changed and outfitted for immortality (The Scofield Memorial Church of Dallas has made good use of the phrase "We shall not all sleep, but we shall all be changed," placing it in the church nursery.)

The triumph of mighty Joshua at Jericho is a type of the Rapture of the Church. There, the people shouted and blew on trumpets, and the walls fell down, and each man "ascended up" into the city. Beautiful Jericho, with its flower gardens and citrus fruits, is a gorgeous oasis in a very arid wilderness. It was the place where God chose to take His people into their Promised Land. It was their first sight of anything but hopeless desert for some forty years. Likewise, with the Christians, our glimpse of heaven at the Rapture will represent the end of a long journey for each of us through the wilderness. The entire story of the exodus — the story of Passover, our first feast — illustrates the salvation of the believer. First, there was the blood of the lamb, which delivered him from death, then the trip through the Red Sea — baptism, then the wandering in the wilderness — this life on earth, and finally, Jericho — heaven, when the trumpets sound. There is a very close comparison between the verses, Joshua 6:5 and I Thes. 4:16-17, as if God purposely indicated the correlation. If the Israelites could believe that their exalted group of men, women, and children could cross the Jordan and assault mighty Jericho, with its huge walls, and somehow take the city, then the Christian can equally believe that he can rise off the earth and meet the Lord in the air. The clincher of the type is in the name of the leader; in both cases, Joshua (Jesus' name was, of course, Yeshua, in Hebrew, Joshua, in English.)

Sadly, only a small portion of the Jews (the remnant which is in the Church at the time of the Rapture) will see this magnificent fulfillment. Jeremiah, with his usual clear-eyed forecast, lamented the situation:

> The harvest is past, the summer is ended, and we are not saved (Jer. 8:20).

But for the remaining Jews of the world, who will not participate in the Rapture of the Church, God will have a restoration to the Promised Land. We have seen a portion of the Jews retake the land, of course, but Isaiah indicates that they will *all* go back at the sound of the trumpet:

> And it shall come to pass in that day, that the Lord shall beat off from the channel of the river unto the stream of Egypt, and ye shall be gathered one by one, O ye children of Israel. And it shall come to pass in that day, that the great trumpet shall be blown, and they shall come which were ready to perish in the land of Assyria and the outcast in the land of Egypt, and shall worship the Lord in the holy mount at Jerusalem (Isaiah 27:12-13).

We might suppose this would be a logical move for Jews left on earth after the Church is gone, in the tribulation period. The Jewish people will hardly have a friend anywhere. They certainly won't bow to the Antichrist, particularly when he enters the Temple (II Thes. 2:3-4), and their best defense will be to stand back-to-back with their brethren in the Holy Land. This is how it will happen that the Lord will find them all regathered when He returns (Romans 11:26).

Trumpets, then, occurs on the seventh new moon of the year, a significant time for the conclusion of an age. The Church will be taken out of the world, and God will move on to the difficult fulfillment of the next and most sacred of Jewish feasts.

ATONEMENT

On the fearsome Day of Atonement, the Jew literally either lived or died, according to God's will:

Also on the tenth day of this seventh month there shall be a day of atonement: it shall be an holy convocation unto you; and ye shall afflict your souls, and offer an offering made by fire unto the Lord (Lev. 23:27).

This was a day of confession and it still is. Israel was to individually "afflict their souls" and be conscious of their national sin. This was the day on which the High Priest of Israel entered the fearsome Holy of Holies, where God Himself dwelt (Lev. 16). The high priest would make a sacrifice on his own behalf, and then a sacrifice on behalf of all the sins of all the Israelites. It was a most solemn occasion, still treated as the highest of the holy days. We might appreciate some of the difficult laws written right into Lev. 23, along with the punishments involved with this sacred day:

And ye shall do no work in that same day: for it is a day of atonement, to make an atonement for you before the Lord your God. For whatsoever soul it be that shall not be afflicted in that same day, he shall be cut off from among his people. And whatsoever soul it be that doeth any work in that same day, the same soul will I destroy from among his people (Lev. 23:28-30).

For the slightest violation in terms of working that day (lifting something too heavy, walking too far), one could be cut off from his people, and thus no longer be chosen. Further trips to the Temple would be unnecessary, as redemption would then be hopeless. As to the confession time, God specified twenty-four hours:

> It shall be unto you a sabbath of rest, and ye shall afflict your souls: in the ninth day of the month at even, from even unto even, shall ye celebrate your sabbath (Lev. 23:32).

We might all balk at the terrible thought of twenty-four solid hours of confession, but then the Jews were confessing the sins of an entire year. We might even balk at the idea of merely staying awake for twenty-four hours, but if our salvation hung in the balance, we would try to make it. Such were the blessings and curses of God's own people.

We would look in vain in the New Testament for a fulfillment for the Day of Atonement. This is the one feast which is not fulfilled by the Church, because the Church owes no atonement. The Church is not innocent of course, but it is exonerated. Jesus paid off the sins of every one of us. But these are Jewish feasts, and each one is fulfilled for the Jews. The Day of Atonement will be fulfilled in a wonderful way when the Lord returns at His second coming. Zechariah's marvelous poetry pictured the reaction of Israel to the very sight of the King of the Jews returning:

> And I will pour upon the house of David, and upon the inhabitants of Jerusalem, the spirit of grace and of supplication: and they shall look upon me whom they have pierced, and they shall mourn for him, as one mourneth for his only son, and shall be in bitterness for him, as one that is in bitterness for his firstborn (Zechariah 12:10).

> In that day there shall be a fountain opened to the house of David and to the inhabitants of Jerusalem for sin and for uncleanness (Zechariah 13:1).

How sorrowful Israel will feel indeed, in the presence of their King:

> And one shall say unto him, What are these wounds in thine hands? Then he shall answer, Those with which I was wounded in the house of my friends (Zechariah 13:6).

But the atonement will be accepted. God will have at long last ended His separation from Israel, His original wife. The book of Hosea details the adultery of Israel, in type, and her final redemption and purification. Paul's words bear repeating:

> And so all Israel shall be saved: as it is written, There shall come out of Sion the Deliverer, and shall turn away ungodliness from Jacob. (Romans 11:26).

Sometimes Christians are confused by preaching that indicates "All the Jews will be saved anyway, so why should we bother witnessing to them now?" This would be an erroneous reading of Scripture, since only *surviving* Israel will be saved when the Lord returns. A man who dies now before being saved, Jew or Gentile, cannot obtain salvation in the future, and we should note that it will be very difficult for little Israel to survive the tribulation in any great numbers. The prophets lament that two-thirds of that nation shall perish at the hands of the Antichrist.

TABERNACLES

The prophetic picture becomes much brighter with the happy occasion of the seventh feast:

> Speak unto the children of Israel, saying, The fifteenth day of this seventh month shall be the feast of tabernacles for seven days unto the Lord (Lev. 23:34).

God wanted to celebrate the fact that He provided shelter for the Israelites in the wilderness:

> Ye shall dwell in booths seven days; all that are Israelites born shall dwell in booths: That your generations may know that I made the children of Israel to dwell in booths, when I brought them out of the land of Egypt: I am the Lord your God (Lev. 23:42-43).

Each year on Tabernacles, the fifteenth day of the seventh month, or the seventh full moon of the year, devout Jews build little shelters outside their houses, and worship in them. In Jerusalem, a municipal shelter is provided near the Jaffa Gate for the whole of the city.

Tabernacles represents, of course, the Lord's shelter in the world to come, His great Tabernacle to exist in Jerusalem during the Kingdom Age. This seventh feast, commemorated faithfully by Jesus (John 7), is the one feast that we are assured will be an important part of kingdom worship:

> And it shall come to pass, that every one that is left of all the nations which come against Jerusalem shall even go up from year to year to worship the King, the Lord of hosts, and to keep the Feast of Tabernacles.
>
> And it shall be, that whoso will not come up of all the families of the earth unto Jerusalem to worship the King, the Lord of hosts, even upon them shall be no rain.
>
> And if the families of Egypt go not up, and come not, that have no rain; there shall be the plague, wherewith the Lord will smite the heathen that comes not up to keep the feast of tabernacles.
>
> This shall be the punishment of Egypt, and the punishment of all nations that come not up to keep the feast of tabernacles (Zechariah 14:16-19).

The Lord will establish His Tabernacle in Jerusalem (Ezekiel 37:26-27), and all the world will come every year to appear before the King and worship Him. How fitting a conclusion to each festival year in the schedule of the feasts!

SOME CONCLUSIONS

Now after looking over the feasts, it becomes very clear that God did a momentous thing here. He forecast the entire career of the Messiah, the Jews, the Church, and even the other nations. He foresaw the tribulation period in all its agony, the presence of the Jew and the Gentile together in the Church, and even the detail of leaving the corners of the fields for sustenance for the poor, including His Son and His disciples.

He laid out the feasts in the calendar year in a manner that reflects in proportion the history of the Church. Indeed, those first three feasts, the crucifixion, burial, and resurrection, occurred very close together. Then there was the pause before the coming of the Holy Spirit. And then the long pause before the big harvest, the Rapture of the Church.

The seven feasts reassure us about a pre-tribulation Rapture. Surely the entire system would be wrecked if the Church were not to be rewarded at Trumpets, but would have to put in an unwarranted Day of Atonement with unbelieving Israel in the tribulation period. We may also see God's clever design shown in the earthly week — six feasts of work and the last one of rest. It is rather like the creation week, in which God worked six days and then relaxed in His Tabernacle on the seventh. The biblical history has indeed described some six thousand years, and if we are to foresee the kingdom, somewhere in the near future, then a logical one thousand year rest period is coming up.

It is possible that we can even pinpoint the day of the Antichrist's blasphemy in the Temple at Jerusalem during the tribulation period. Since we saw that the tribulation period ends on the Day of Atonement (the Second Coming), then it must have started seven years before on the Day of Atonement. Since the Day of Atonement is on the tenth day of the seventh month, and since the Antichrist comes exactly in the midst of the tribulation period (Daniel 9:27; Rev. 11:1-3), then the day of the blasphemy is at the exact 3½ year point, or the tenth day of the first month in the fourth year. Is there something significant about the tenth day of the first month? Well, that is four days before Passover, which is on the 14th. God asked the Jews to select their sacrificial lamb in Egypt exactly four days before Passover (Exodus 12:3), in order that they examine the lamb for blemishes before sacrificing it on Passover day. The Lord Himself appropriately observed this detail, riding the donkey into Jerusalem on Palm Sunday, four days before Passover, so that the people might examine Him before choosing Him as their lamb. Thus we see the Antichrist will make the perfect counterfeit, arriving at the Temple four days before Passover and presenting himself as Almighty God. The way we discern the true God from a false one is that Jesus Christ rode the donkey in humility, and the Antichrist comes claiming that he is God Incarnate!

Many other such intricate computations can be made from the schedule of the seven feasts, but they are not always successful. People have tried to calculate the date of the Rapture, or the Kingdom, from the system, or tried to place historical events in perspective of the feasts. It seems that either the Scriptures have yielded as yet too little to our poor scrutiny, or that such details are purposely concealed from us.

Nevertheless, a working knowledge of this marvelous prophetic system builds the faith of any Bible reader, and certainly of the believers in Jesus Christ.

II
"UNTO US A CHILD IS BORN"

A most intriguing and almost startling application of the system of the seven feasts came my way recently during some research for a book. Perhaps this whimsical little section will serve as an example of how God's formulas pervade this earthly, human life.

I was asked by one of my publishers to look into writing a book about the birth of a baby from a biblical perspective. The book was to be a gift book to be presented to Christian couples at arrival of blessed events.

This pleasant assignment led me to the many fascinating birth stories in the Bible, including, of course, the wondrous birth of our Lord. But I preferred to do more than just celebrate a new arrival; there are many adequate books for such purposes. Rather I wanted to find some theological principle, perhaps some hidden truth in the Scriptures, about how each of us are born. I wanted to know if the Scriptures held some secret as to how God makes us.

To that end I contacted Dr. Margaret Matheson, a Bible-reading friend, and a very good obstetrician who has delivered over ten thousand babies.

I questioned Margaret about pregnancy in general, how it is calculated, and how the baby develops within the mother. I learned that the average pregnancy is 280 days and is counted from the first day of the last menstrual cycle before conception. Making calculations on the Jewish calendar is rather a hobby of mine, and I placed this 280 days on an "ideal Jewish year." The ideal Jewish year would start exactly at the spring equinox, with the first day of Nisan, the new moon of the first month, occurring on the first day of spring, March 21st. Interesting, I found that a pregnancy of 280 days, begun on March 21, would end on a very interesting date, December 25. We don't know if Christmas Day was actually the date of the birth of our Lord, but we do know that Kislev is the accurate date of Chanukah, the Feast of Dedication, which our Lord did commemorate (John 10:22). That discovery led me to think that there must be something very biblical indeed about the pregnancy term, and I asked Margaret for more details.

It was really Margaret's first statement that turned me on to the whole system I'm about to disclose. I asked Margaret to tell me in some detail just how the baby is made and how it grows, and she began with this statement: "On the fourteenth day of the first month, the egg appears." I couldn't help hearing that familiar ring of Lev. 23:5: "In the fourteenth day of the first month . . .", God's original instruction for the observance of Passover. The Jews use an egg on the Passover table as symbolic of the new life they were granted by the sacrifice of the lamb in Egypt. The egg, of course, appears in the Easter celebration as well, symbolic of the same thing, although not from biblical sources, as we have seen. The egg is an appropriate enough man-made symbol of a new life, and I was fascinated that the fourteenth day of a pregnancy does the same thing as the fourteenth day of God's festival year: It brings the chance of new life.

I was already thinking in my mind that the baby must develop along the schedule of the seven feasts, but I concealed my excitement from Margaret. I didn't want to encourage her to slant the facts in any way, just to prove a biblical point. I questioned her carefully, keeping in mind that the next feast, Unleavened Bread, must occur the very next night, the fifteenth day of the first month, according to Lev. 23:6. I asked Margaret how soon fertilization of the mother's egg must occur if pregnancy is to happen.

Her answer was very clear and very definite. "Fertilization must occur within twenty-four hours or the egg will pass on."

Now I was getting excited. Not only did the two momentous prenatal events occur on the right days, but they were also the appropriate events. The egg, of course, for Passover, and the idea of fertilization — the planting of the seed — for Unleavened Bread, the burial of our Lord. His crucifixion on Passover gave each of us the chance for life everlasting. His burial in the earth, prepared for each of us, the glorious resurrection to come.

I almost held my breath as I inquired about First Fruits. I realized that this third feast is not on a definite time cycle. It simply occurs on the Sunday during the week of Unleavened Bread. It could be the day after, or it could be almost a week away. I asked Margaret cautiously what happened next in the birth process.

"Well, that's a little bit indeterminate," she said. "The fertilized egg travels down the tube at its own speed toward the uterus. It may take anywhere from two to six days before it implants."

I loved her word "implants" because it so suggested the festival of First Fruits, the spring planting, and it was the correct technical term, I found out. The medical term is "implantation." This marks the moment when the fertilized egg arrives safely in the uterus and begins its miraculous growth into a human being.

Needless to say, Margaret and I were very soon occupied with a pile of obstetrical textbooks, embryonic charts, and, of course, the Scriptures in several translations. I appealed to her to help me track this thing down, but I still did not disclose to her just what I was after. I was only going to ask her about how our little fertilized egg would develop, without telling her that I fully expected a very exact schedule in accordance with the feasts.

It's probably not necessary for me to say that I was holding my breath by this time, in hopes that something had really been uncovered. After all, it was so beautiful so far. Surely God designed the conception of each of us in accordance with those first three majestic feasts, so appropriately fulfilled by our Lord.

But would the system continue? The next one was the tough one. It seemed that things were happening fast on the pregnancy schedule, but the seven feasts' schedule now called for that long wait until Pentecost. I asked Margaret cautiously what the next development would be with our implanted egg.

"Well, of course, we have a slowly developing embryo here for a long time," she said. "It goes through stages, but there's really no dramatic change until it becomes an actual fetus. That's the next big event. You can see it all right here on the chart." And she turned her medical book toward me so that I could see a page divided like a calendar, showing the first few weeks of the embryonic development.

I looked across the little pictures at what seemed like a little tadpole, which soon had flippers, and then began to look like a little man from Mars, and so on down to the very last picture on the page. There I saw a human baby, and beside that drawing, the very scriptural message, "Fifty days."

I looked up at Margaret, trying to conceal my excitement, and said carefully, "Is the fiftieth day important?"

"Well," said the obstetrician, "Up until the fiftieth day you wouldn't know if you're going to have a duck or a cocker spaniel. But at the fiftieth day of the embryo, it becomes a human fetus."

Scriptural phrases were flying through my head. "A new creature" seemed to be the appropriate one for the momentous event of the change from this indiscriminate life form, the embryo, to what was essentially a human being. Indeed, on that day of Pentecost, those as yet unregenerate Israelites at the Temple became truly "new creatures". They became spiritual. They received life eternal. They were not the same now as they were before (II Cor. 5:17). They would now go on to another life outside the confines of the fleshy bodies they were in, in the manner that that fetus would go on to another life outside the body of its mother.

Margaret apprised me that every scheduled event in the birth of the baby varied somewhat with the particular case, just as the length of the entire pregnancy would vary from mother to mother. The medical book chart had measured its fifty days from fertilization, rather than from implantation (First Fruits in the Scriptures), but the variations among pregnancies would account for the difference. Substantially, after the seventh week, following conception, this embryo — this inhuman life form — would become that one creature created in God's own image.

I next asked Margaret about the first day of the seventh month. I had hoped that there were no big events through what would be the long summer on the schedule of the feasts, and indeed, there were none. It seemed that the fetus, once started on its growth into a human being ready to be born, progressed in a rather general way with nothing momentous happening. The baby, I now realized, had developed very early and now was only gaining size and strength. But, of course, there were a few small perfections to be added by the hand of the Creator, and I was delighted to find that one of these coincided so exactly with the next feast.

The perfection that arrived just at the beginning of the seventh month, was the baby's hearing. Margaret's medical textbooks, including the definitive *Williams Obstetrics*, stated that the baby's hearing was now fully developed. At the first day of the seventh month, the baby could discriminate a sound for what it really was. For example, a trumpet was a trumpet! Just in time for the Lord to descend from heaven with a shout and with the sound of the trump of God, that baby could perceive the sounds!

I was now out for blood — that is, the blood that would represent the sixth feast, the Day of Atonement. This was the outstanding day of blood sacrifice, and I specified to Margaret that I wanted to know if there was any development just ten days into the seventh month. I still was careful not to imply just what I was looking for. If Margaret had said, "The elbows are finished," then I suppose my system would have been finished. But somehow I was very confident by now, and the obstetrician didn't let me down.

Half quoting from her textbook, and concentrating hard, Margaret stated that the important changes now indeed were in the blood. It was necessary for the fetal blood, which carried the mother's oxygen through the baby's system, to change in such a way that the baby could carry the oxygen that it, itself, would obtain upon birth. Technically, the hemoglobin of the blood would have to change from that of the fetus to that of a self-respirating and circulating human being. The fetus does not breathe, but rather depends on the oxygen obtained through the mother's blood circulation. Naturally, this system must be changed before birth, and that change occurred, according to Margaret's textbooks, in the second week of the seventh month, and to be precise, on the tenth day!

"The blood acceptable" rang through my mind. "I have given you the blood for remission of sin" (Lev. 17:11), was God's statement. Indeed, each person of Israel had to present blood to the Lord through the high priest of Israel on the Day of Atonement. If that blood was acceptable, then there would be life. Likewise, in the fetus, when that blood was mature, there would be life.

But, of course, the fetus is not ready to be born. There

remained still another feast, and by this time I was quite confident that Margaret would come up with the appropriate fulfillment. I asked for the fifteenth day of the seventh month, and she immediately recognized the date as the beginning of the safe delivery period.

"You see, that's when the lungs are developed," she said, "And as long as they get their little lungs going, we can bring them along, even if they are born at that early time. I'm afraid if they decide to come before those lungs are finished, then they have very little chance. But by the fifteenth day of the seventh month, a normal baby has two healthy lungs, and if born at that point, can take in its own air and live on it."

The Feast of Tabernacles, I pondered, but, of course, the Tabernacle is the house of the spirit, the spirit is the air in the Bible! Didn't God blow breath into Adam to make him live? Didn't Christ breathe the Holy Spirit upon His disciples? And even more so, in Ezekiel's dry bones vision, (Ezekiel 37) Ezekiel saw God make dead bones, sinews, and muscles come together into human beings, and then commanded the prophet, "Then said he unto me, Prophesy unto the wind, prophesy, son of man, and say to the wind, Thus saith the Lord God; Come from four winds, O breath, and breathe upon these slain, that they may live." (Ezekiel 37:9)

Tabernacles is the end of the road — the end of the feasts, the end of God's plan, the beginning of the kingdom. The baby would live if born at Tabernacles. The believer will live once he enters the kingdom.

THE ETERNAL LIGHT

I followed this system still further, even though I had seen in God's feasts on Mt. Sinai, the birth of each one of us. There is still the full 280-day period to consider, which leads to the actual normal birthtime. I now had such confidence in the logic of the Bible, that I took out my Jewish calendar again and worked with the added Festival of Dedication, Chanukah. It was not given by God on Mount Sinai, but was prophesied by Daniel (Daniel 8:9-14), and took place in 165 B.C. when the Temple was rededicated.

The nature of Chanukah has to do with the eternal light in the Temple (and in every synagogue today). God had made a great miracle on the occasion when Antiochus entered the Temple and sacrificed a sow on the altar. The Macabees threw him out but found only one precious can of consecrated oil — a day's supply — with which to maintain the eternal light. A great miracle answered their prayers, however. The oil lasted eight days and sustained the light until more was ready. And so the Jews still light a candle each night for eight nights on the Feast of Chanukah.

I found what I fully expected on the Jewish calendar. Chanukah lies just the right distance beyond Tabernacles to account for the actual birth of the baby. The 280 days, it occurred to me while working with the Jewish calendar, expressed exactly ten of those mysterious twenty-eight day cycles of the moon, a system more in keeping with the way God would plan things than our Western nine-month pregnancy estimate. In any case, the eight day period of Chanukah accounted for even the off-schedule births, for the most part, and this added festival clearly left a great symbol to the whole system. Beyond Tabernacles — beyond the Kingdom — we have eternity with God. This then is the fulfillment of the eternal light.

THE BIRTH OF A KING

All of the above conclusions are given just as I found them out, researching with a friend, the obstetrician. No attempt has been made in a book of this space to create precision medical charts on technical calendars and so forth. I hope to leave that to more scientific minds who could do it justice. But I doubt if a flaw would be found, since we are dealing here with God's Word, and that is the first important point about this interesting discovery.

It shows that the Bible is not just somebody's poetry or somebody's mythology. We don't have to shrink back, defensively claiming that we just "believe" in the Word on something like this. I watched with deep respect as the doctor carefully copied the dates of the seven feasts from the book of Leviticus into her own obstetrical textbooks, so that she might more carefully follow the pregnancies of her patients in the future. I saw that she totally believed some things she had not seen before in all of the time that she had monitored all of those pregnancies. I saw that what God said on Mount Sinai is effective today, useful in a scientific way. More than that, I also saw that each of us has fulfilled the seven feasts in a unique way, before we were actually born! Certainly, each of us developed along the schedule of the feasts, as explained above. In the theory of evolution, it is taught that the embryo and fetus describe some series of past development through other species, which finally produced the human being. But Margaret put into plain words that the explanation of the seven feasts was much better, and the other thing never appealed to her scientifically, in any case. Rather, we can see the Creator, efficient as He is, using certain structures from organism to organism, and with His masterpiece, Man, using this magnificent calendar of festival occasions and prophetic fulfillments, in the assembly and development of each of these special creatures.

Whether we know the feasts or not, we each accomplished every one of them!

And finally, in a great and cosmic way, we are watching Jesus "being born" as King. We saw Him born on earth as the Lamb of God, and His life was quickly snuffed out, but not before His grand purpose was accomplished. But in a greater way, we are to see Him come as King when the great Feast of Tabernacles arrives for all of the believers. Thus we have seen our Lord progress through Passover, Unleavened Bread, First Fruits and Pentecost. We shall see Him, soon we pray, in that Feast of Trumpets, and we shall return with Him on the day of Atonement. But His complete birth cycle, as it were, will see Him crowned as the rightful King of this creation, when that final Tabernacles is reached.

Each of us will then begin that magnificent life with God that we are promised, and our Lord will begin the kingly reign He has so patiently forestalled while we work in His fields.

GOD'S WILL

I thought all of the above would make a superb book, but surprisingly, the publisher turned it down. It had taken a long time to amass the material and present it in book publisher form and the company's interest had moved elsewhere. I tried it on a second and third publisher, with little effect.

I was confused by this. Why would God close a door through which so much light had come? I finally concluded that I would write the material as I have here, in one of these little study guides which I produce myself. However, as the year of 1978 went on, I kept putting off the task.

I kept feeling God's hints and proddings right along. Wasn't this one of those "perfect years" when Chanukah and Christmas arrived together? Wouldn't this be a fitting year for this book? But I stood around like the reluctant Gideon, seemingly waiting for more of a sign. Finally, God let me have it, and in His typically appropriate way.

My wife became pregnant!

God's will is God's will. I have finally sat down to write! And Baby Boy or Girl Levitt will arrive, if that is God's will, in

February of 1979. And if I said these words very close to his secure home in his mother's tummy, he would hear them, I know, because he has just passed his first Feast of Trumpets. Next week God will change my baby's blood and make it acceptable, and the week after that, He will provide him those tabernacles of the Spirit, the lungs.

May we all hear our Father's voice, as he discloses to us, the things that are His in His Word.

JEWISH FEAST	CHRISTIAN FULFILLMENT	DEVELOPMENT OF A BABY
PASSOVER	New Life (Egg)	Ovulation
UNLEAVENED BREAD	The Seed	Fertilization
FIRST FRUITS	Resurrection	Implantation
PENTECOST	Harvest	New Creature (Fetus)
TRUMPETS	Rapture	Hearing
ATONEMENT	Redemption	Blood (Hemoglobin A)
TABERNACLES	Kingdom	Lungs
CHANUKAH	Eternity	Eternal Life

STUDY BOOK SERIES by Zola Levitt

THE MIRACLE OF PASSOVER:

A complete explanation of the beautiful symbols and shadows of the Messiah which appear in this crown jewel of Jewish Holy Days. The true meaning of Communion as the Lord instituted it and as the Church practices it.

THE SPIRIT OF PENTECOST:

From the fear and trembling of the Upper Room to the magnificent miracle of the coming of the Holy Spirit. An exciting presentation of the full meaning of "the birthday of the Church."

A CHRISTIAN LOVE STORY:

The Jewish wedding customs of the Messiah's time and how He fulfilled them all in calling out His Bride, the Church. A new and deeper understanding of the bond between the Bridegroom and each believer — a spiritual "Love Story".

THE SIGNS OF THE END:

The Messiah's own words of warning about the conditions that would prevail in the world at the end of God's plan. Are we now approaching the Great Tribulation and the return of our King?

GLORY: The Future of the Believers:

The entire prophetic system explained for those who are going to live it! The Rapture, our time in Heaven, the Kingdom and eternity. Where we go from here. Our rewards, our eternal lives, our entire future.

THE SEVEN FEASTS OF ISRAEL:

A complete explanation of the holy days God gave Moses on Mount Sinai, and how each was fulfilled by our Lord. Passover, Pentecost, Trumpets, Tabernacles, etc., fully discussed as to their hidden meanings in the Messiah. A very special section on how every baby in the womb develops according to God's system of the holy days.

THE SECOND COMING:

The prime difference between the biblical faith and worldly religions is that with the Messiah we have a bright future. What we see is not all we get. The life in this world is of little importance to those who have been promised the Kingdom to come. The return of the King fully explained.

SEVEN CHURCHES: Does Yours Fit In?:

A refreshing and unusual perspective on the churches presented in Revelation 2 and 3. A Jewish Christian and Bible scholar, Zola looks at these earliest churches from the Old Testament and Jewish traditional point of view. A highly interesting and most useful study, applicable to church life everywhere today.

HOW CAN A GENTILE BE SAVED?:

Christians always ask Zola, "How did you come to the Lord?" Their **real** question is, "How can a Jew be saved?" He finally decided to make a biblical inquiry into how **they** got saved. The results are extremely thought-provoking.

"IN MY FATHER'S HOUSE":

The Lord said, "In my Father's house are many mansions . . . I go to prepare a place for you." An explanation of the incredible seven years we will spend as guests in heaven, in the Messiah's Father's house.

ISRAEL, MY PROMISED:

Has God finished with the Jews? Are the modern Israelites the valid Chosen People of the Bible? A sensitive and very personal look at the land of our Lord, as seen today and as promised in the Kingdom.